Great Artists

Great Artists
Norman Rockwell

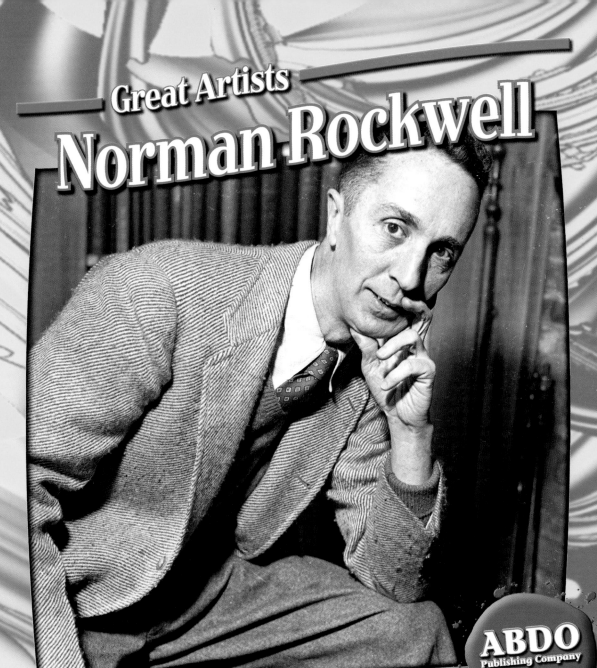

ABDO
Publishing Company

Adam G. Klein

visit us at
www.abdopublishing.com

Published by ABDO Publishing Company, 4940 Viking Drive, Edina, Minnesota 55435.
Copyright © 2007 by Abdo Consulting Group, Inc. International copyrights reserved in all
countries. No part of this book may be reproduced in any form without written permission
from the publisher. The Checkerboard Library™ is a trademark and logo of ABDO Publishing
Company.

Printed in the United States.

Cover Photo: Corbis
Interior Photos: Art Resource p. 27; Bridgeman Art Library p. 11; Corbis pp. 1, 5, 19, 23, 25, 26,
    29; Curtis Publishing pp. 9, 15, 17, 21; Getty Images p. 13
Norman Rockwell artwork p. 9 © 1934 SEPS; p. 15 © 1939 SEPS; p. 17 © 1960 SEPS; p. 21
    © 1948 SEPS; p. 23 © 1943 SEPS: Licensed by Curtis Publishing, Indianapolis, IN. All
    rights reserved. www.curtispublishing.com
Works by Norman Rockwell printed by permission of the Norman Rockwell Family Agency
    Copyright © 2006 the Norman Rockwell Family Entities

Series Coordinator: Megan M. Gunderson
Editors: Rochelle Baltzer, Megan M. Gunderson
Cover Design: Neil Klinepier
Interior Design: Dave Bullen

Library of Congress Cataloging-in-Publication Data

Klein, Adam G., 1976-
  Norman Rockwell / Adam G. Klein.
     p. cm. -- (Great artists)
  Includes index.
   ISBN-10 1-59679-738-X
   ISBN-13 978-1-59679-738-3
  1. Rockwell, Norman, 1894-1978--Juvenile literature. 2. Painters--United States--Biography--
Juvenile literature. 3. Illustrators--United States--Biography--Juvenile literature. I. Rockwell,
Norman, 1894-1978. II. Title III. Series: Klein, Adam G., 1976- . Great artists.

ND237.R68K54 2006
759.13--dc22
                                                                                    2005017896

Contents

Norman Rockwell

Many people consider Norman Rockwell one of the most popular American artists of the 1900s. His illustrated characters bring charm to everyday events. Millions of people can easily relate to these characters. Rockwell's illustrations help many people escape to a more lighthearted place.

Rockwell is best known for illustrating covers for the *Saturday Evening Post*. His paintings show scenes of small-town America with realistic detail, humor, and warmth. Sometimes his characters are carefree, and sometimes they struggle. Rockwell's work connected with many people as he tried to define his American ideal.

The artist behind these images has an interesting story of his own. Rockwell was a **workaholic**. And, he was very insecure. He struggled for perfection throughout his entire career. Rockwell painted the life he wanted. In this way, he lived out his dreams on paper.

Rockwell completed more than 300 covers for the Saturday Evening Post. Some say that Rockwell's works were "as precious to them as their own memories."

Timeline

1894 ~ On February 3, Norman Percevel Rockwell was born in New York City, New York.

1908 ~ Rockwell studied at the Chase School of Art.

1909 ~ Rockwell studied at the National Academy of Design.

1910 ~ Rockwell transferred to the Art Students League.

1912 ~ Rockwell began working for *Boys' Life* magazine.

1916 ~ *Boy with Baby Carriage*, Rockwell's first cover illustration for the *Saturday Evening Post*, appeared on May 20.

1935 ~ Rockwell was asked to illustrate *The Adventures of Tom Sawyer* and *The Adventures of Huckleberry Finn*.

1936 ~ Rockwell completed his only mural, *Yankee Doodle*.

1943 ~ *Freedom of Speech*, *Freedom to Worship*, *Freedom from Want*, and *Freedom from Fear* appeared in the *Saturday Evening Post*; in May, a fire destroyed Rockwell's studio.

1964 ~ *The Problem We All Live With* appeared in *Look* magazine.

1965 ~ *Southern Justice* appeared in *Look* magazine.

1977 ~ Rockwell received the Presidential Medal of Freedom.

1978 ~ Rockwell died on November 3.

Fun Facts

- The Louvre in Paris, France, was Norman Rockwell's favorite museum.

- Rockwell illustrated the annual Boy Scout calendar from 1924 to 1976.

- In 1948, Rockwell designed a line of Christmas cards for Hallmark.

- Rockwell's years in Vermont are generally considered his most fruitful. He produced many paintings that mirrored life in Vermont. There, he found people he felt most comfortable drawing.

- Rockwell and Mary Rhodes Barstow enjoyed many of the same things. She would read Charles Dickens and other authors aloud to Rockwell while he painted. They also attended square dances together.

- During a winter retreat in California in the late 1940s, Rockwell was invited to teach at the Los Angeles Art Institute. He enjoyed working with the young students and found the experience very fulfilling.

The Boy

Norman Percevel Rockwell was born on February 3, 1894, in New York City, New York. His father, Waring Rockwell, worked for a **textile** company. His mother, Anne Mary Hill, was the daughter of an artist.

When Norman was very young, his father taught him to draw. Norman, his older brother Jerry, and their father spent many nights in their home copying magazine pictures. Norman became especially good. Neighborhood children often asked him to draw things for them.

Even though he got along well with others, Norman was sad. Norman wasn't athletic, and he thought that he looked awkward. And, his mother was overprotective of him.

Norman escaped from his life by drawing the characters of his favorite author, Charles Dickens. He imagined himself as a figure in the stories. He wanted a different life.

"God bless us every one," said Tiny Tim

© 1934 SEPS

When Rockwell became a magazine illustrator, he recalled his early love of Charles Dickens. He painted Tiny Tim and Bob Cratchit for the Post in 1934.

What to Do?

In 1907, the Rockwell family moved from New York City to nearby Mamaroneck, New York. The move suited Norman, who enjoyed the more rural surroundings. He felt New York City was becoming too violent and depressing.

Norman was much happier in the country. The boys of the town found him likable and friendly. Norman mowed lawns and delivered mail to earn money. He also gave art lessons to the famous actress Ethel Barrymore. Finding what he liked to do best, Norman decided that he wanted to study art.

In 1908, Norman started to take a few classes at the Chase School of Art. In 1909, he left Mamaroneck High School in order to attend the National Academy of Design. In 1910, Norman transferred to the Art Students League. There, he finally found a program that he liked.

When Rockwell painted, he often focused on simple situations and small-town life.

Illustrating

Norman appreciated works by classical artists such as Rembrandt, Pieter Bruegel, and Johannes Vermeer. But, he also liked the work of illustrators such as Howard Pile and J.C. Leyendecker. So, he decided to pursue a career as an illustrator.

Early influences on Norman's artistic style included two of his teachers at the Art Students League. There, Norman studied **anatomy** with George Bridgman and illustration with Thomas Fogarty. Fogarty also helped Norman get his first **commission**.

Norman worked so hard in school he hardly had time for anything else. But, all of Norman's studying paid off. In 1912, he got his first professional assignment. He was only 18 years old! Norman soon found himself with more jobs than he could handle.

Later that year, Norman began working for *Boys' Life* magazine. He also provided illustrations for several other well-known juvenile magazines. At the age of 19, he was named art editor for *Boys' Life*. Over six years, Norman produced about 400 illustrations for the magazine.

Rockwell is known for his Boy Scout illustrations.
This image was eventually used on a postage stamp.

A New Direction

Rockwell worried that he would be creating children's illustrations for the rest of his life. He wanted a different challenge. So, he traveled to Philadelphia, Pennsylvania. He was hoping to find work at the *Saturday Evening Post*. One of his heroes, Leyendecker, worked for that magazine.

Without making an appointment, Rockwell arrived at the magazine's headquarters. His art was taken to the *Post*'s editor, George Lorimer. Lorimer was impressed and bought two of Rockwell's paintings to use as covers for the magazine. Rockwell's first cover illustration appeared May 20, 1916. It was titled *Boy with Baby Carriage*.

Soon after Rockwell's sale to the *Post*, he met schoolteacher Irene O'Connor. He proposed to her almost immediately. The couple married on July 1, 1916. They moved to New Rochelle, New York, where Rockwell was surrounded by other illustrators.

In 1918, Rockwell briefly joined the U.S. Navy. He was stationed in Charleston, South Carolina, where he worked on newspaper **layouts** and cartoons. He never saw active duty, and he returned home after only a few months.

Rockwell picked up some advertising jobs for additional income. He found it difficult to turn down jobs. Again, he became swamped with work. He was unable to enjoy his success because he was so busy! At the age of 25, he already felt worn out.

Rockwell painted America's national pastime, baseball, several times for the Post. *As with any of his works, the facial expression of each character helps convey the feeling of the scene.*

Working Years

Rockwell painted scenes of the average person's daily life. He used live models as his subjects. The models enjoyed working with Rockwell. They said he was very pleasant, and he made them feel important to his process.

Through his work, Rockwell had made many friends in New Rochelle. And, he and his wife could afford to build a house there. Yet, he still was not happy.

Rockwell continued to work long hours. He tried to escape into his paintings, but he needed to escape from his real life. So, Rockwell spent several weeks in Europe. While there, he attended an art school in Paris, France.

Self-Portrait

In Triple Self-Portrait (below), *each of the three Rockwells is different. In the mirror, Rockwell is clearly wearing glasses. But in the drawing, he is not. Rockwell also looks older from behind than he does in either the mirror image or the drawing. Rockwell's autobiography began in this issue of the* Post. *It revealed even more of how the artist saw himself.*

The objects in the painting represent Rockwell. Some are props from other works. Others are simply things he enjoys, such as a glass of Coca-Cola. He has self-portraits by other great artists, such as Rembrandt and Vincent van Gogh, pinned to the side of his canvas. And, he put his signature on the unfinished canvas in the painting, rather than in the bottom right corner of his own finished work.

A New Life

In 1929, Rockwell's wife asked him for a divorce. But, Rockwell wasn't alone for long. He soon met Mary Rhodes Barstow, a schoolteacher. They married on April 17, 1930. Rockwell's family soon grew with the birth of his first son, Jarvis.

Rockwell was a perfectionist and continued to feel unhappy with his work. He wanted to do more than just illustrate covers for the *Post*. He wanted to create something that was timeless.

In 1932, Rockwell attended a showing of the work of **muralist** Diego Rivera. Soon after, Rockwell decided to return to Paris to find inspiration. He wanted to be taken seriously as an artist, not only as an illustrator.

After returning to New Rochelle in 1933, Rockwell's second son, Thomas, was born. Rockwell was still seeking satisfaction from his work. Soon, a project came to him that he thoroughly enjoyed. In 1935, he was asked to illustrate new **editions** of

Mark Twain's *The Adventures of Tom Sawyer* and *The Adventures of Huckleberry Finn*.

It was important to Rockwell to make his work as **authentic** as possible. So, he traveled to Hannibal, Missouri, where the books take place. He bought props to use in the illustrations. And then, he asked local people to pose for him. However, it was at this time that Rockwell stopped working directly from live models. He began illustrating primarily from photographs of them instead.

Rockwell met and married Mary Rhodes Barstow in California.

Vermont

The illustrations for the Twain books were a success. Rockwell felt like his world was back on track. In 1936, he painted his only **mural**, *Yankee Doodle*. It was later hung on the wall of a New Jersey inn.

Also in 1936, Rockwell's third son, Peter, was born. And in 1938, Rockwell decided to move the family to Arlington, Vermont. He was looking for a more solitary place to work.

Arlington was a good fit for Rockwell. There, he made many artist friends and was active in the community. His wife cared for their home and their finances, while Rockwell worked in his studio. Rockwell had many of the local people pose for his pictures.

Rockwell's services were in great demand. His continuing work for the *Post* took up much of his time. In addition, Rockwell took on assignments from other magazines, such as

McCall's. And, he continued to create advertisements for **clients**. As usual, Rockwell took on more work than he could handle. He was forced to work seven days a week to keep up.

Rockwell's wife Mary appears in The Gossips. *This playful painting shows a rumor traveling through town. Rockwell himself is the last accusing person on the page. The rumor is about him!*

Freedom Series

After the start of **World War II**, Rockwell created a fictional character named Willie Gillis. He used Gillis to tell the story of a typical American soldier's life from basic training through the war.

In total, Rockwell created 11 *Post* covers featuring the young soldier. He hoped to make a personal character that people could relate to during the war. Overall, there was positive public support for his Gillis illustrations. Many people liked the covers. However, some soldiers thought that they did not reflect the suffering that they felt.

Rockwell tried to keep politics out of his works. The political paintings that he worked on usually did not take sides. But Rockwell did have his personal beliefs. And soon, a project came to him that he felt driven to complete.

On January 6, 1941, President Franklin D. Roosevelt delivered an impressive speech. He spoke about basic freedoms that everybody

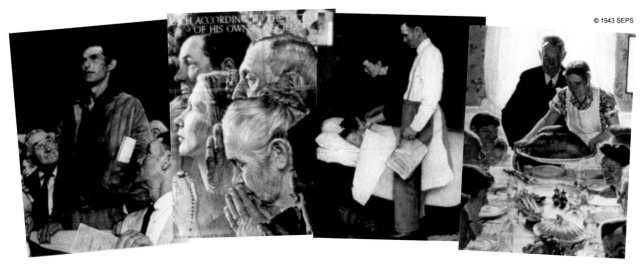

Rockwell didn't decide to paint the Four Freedoms until a year after Roosevelt's speech.

should be able to enjoy. Roosevelt's words inspired Rockwell. So, he decided to transform the freedoms into four illustrative stories.

Freedom of Speech, *Freedom to Worship*, *Freedom from Fear*, and *Freedom from Want* appeared in the *Post* in 1943. The Four Freedoms toured the United States and were seen by more than 1 million people. They raised $133 million in war **bonds** to support the fighting overseas.

Fire

One night in May 1943, Tommy Rockwell noticed a fire coming from his father's studio. The fire quickly destroyed Rockwell's library, his art supplies, and some paintings.

People felt sorry for Rockwell's loss. Fans and fellow illustrators from all over sent Rockwell supplies to replace what he had lost. Rockwell later sketched his version of what happened, and it was published in the *Post*.

Rockwell and his family moved to a new home in West Arlington, Vermont, to start over. Late in 1953, the Rockwells relocated again to Stockbridge, Massachusetts. There, Norman and Mary took art classes in town. No matter how well Rockwell painted, he was always concerned with the quality of his work.

Rockwell's style changed over the years. His paintings became less cartoonish and more realistic. Still, Rockwell always tried to create human emotion in his paintings. His ultimate job as an illustrator was to tell a story.

Artist's Corner

Rockwell was a perfectionist, and usually followed a specific process when creating his artwork. Often, he would begin with either photographs of people in costume or live models in his studio. Sometimes he would pose them, as he is doing with this Ben Franklin model *(below)*. From these, he could create the proper look of his characters. Some of his characters became very familiar, as local townspeople were often portrayed in more than one work.

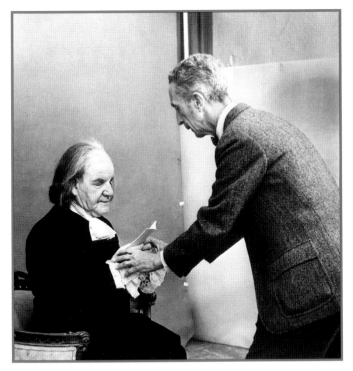

Next, Rockwell would create a charcoal drawing of the work. This early stage allowed him to establish where everything in the picture would fit best. Using this drawing, Rockwell would then create an oil sketch of the work. This helped him decide on colors. After this, Rockwell would create the final painting. He made a pencil tracing of the drawing on his canvas, and then painted over it until he felt the work was complete.

Look

On August 25, 1959, Rockwell's wife Mary Rhodes Barstow died from heart failure. Two years later, he married an ex-schoolteacher, Mary Leete Punderson.

In 1963, the *Post* and Rockwell parted ways. The management felt that the paper needed an updated look. They thought Rockwell was too old-fashioned and sentimental. His last cover for the *Post* was a portrait of Egyptian president Gamal Abdel Nasser.

Rockwell married "Molly" Punderson and became a grandfather all in the same year!

Rockwell painted other political leaders, such as President Richard Nixon.

Soon after leaving the *Post*, Rockwell found a job at *Look* magazine. The people at *Look* allowed Rockwell more artistic freedom.

Rockwell's paintings became more obviously political. His new illustrations for *Look* showed issues of poverty and **racism**. Among these works are *The Problem We All Live With*, which appeared in 1964, and *Southern Justice*, from 1965.

Many Honors

Rockwell continued to work on a variety of projects. When he found time to reflect back on his life, he realized that he was well respected. Then in 1969, the Norman Rockwell Museum opened in Stockbridge, Massachusetts. It became a popular place to visit.

Exhibits of Rockwell's work opened in many other places. And, Rockwell received the Presidential Medal of Freedom in 1977. Rockwell was very honored. He lived his life through his work and painted the stories and history around him.

Eventually, Rockwell started to slow down. His memory started to fail, and he became increasingly weaker. Rockwell died on November 3, 1978, and was buried in Stockbridge.

Rockwell's work continues to be popular today. It can be seen in countless books and advertisements. Thousands of people visit his museum every year. People still relate to his

This is the Old Corner House. It held the Norman Rockwell Museum for 24 years before the collection was moved to a new location in 1993. Today, the museum has the largest collection of Rockwell's work.

work even though so much time has passed. His positive view of the world continues to win him many fans.

Glossary

anatomy - the branch of science that deals with the structure of animals or plants and the relationship of their parts.

authentic - real.

bond - a certificate sold by a government. The certificate promises to pay its purchase price plus interest on or after a given future date.

client - a person who hires or uses the services of a professional of some type.

commission - a request to complete a work, such as a painting, for a certain person. To be commissioned is to be given such a request.

edition - an issue of a publication.

layout - the design or the arrangement of something, especially printed material such as a newspaper or a book.

mural - a picture painted on a wall or a ceiling. A muralist is a person who creates such a work.

racism - the belief that one race is better than another.

textile - of or having to do with the designing, manufacturing, or producing of a woven fabric.

workaholic - a person who feels the need to work excessive amounts.

World War II - from 1939 to 1945, fought in Europe, Asia, and Africa. Great Britain, France, the United States, the Soviet Union, and their allies were on one side. Germany, Italy, Japan, and their allies were on the other side.

Saying It

Gamal Abdel Nasser - juh-MAHL AHB-dul NAHS-uhr

Johannes Vermeer - yoh-HAHN-uhs vuhr-MAYR

Mamaroneck - muh-MAR-uh-nehk

Pieter Bruegel - PEE-tuhr BROO-guhl

Web Sites

To learn more about Norman Rockwell, visit ABDO Publishing Company on the World Wide Web at **www.abdopub.com**. Web sites about Rockwell are featured on our Book Links page. These links are routinely monitored and updated to provide the most current information available.

Index